Elementary Professional Resource Book

Conflict Resolution

High-interest stories that encourage critical thinking, creative writing, and dialogue

Written by

Martha E. Kendall

Cover Design by

Peggy Jackson

Inside Illustrations by

Shauna Mooney Kawasaki

Published by Instructional Fair • TS Denison
an imprint of

McGraw-Hill
Children's Publishing

About the Author

Martha E. Kendall grew up in Rochester, New York. She graduated from the University of Michigan. She earned a master's degree in English from Stanford University and a second master's in Social Science from San José State University. She currently teaches literature and language at San José City College.

In addition to producing college videos and texts, Martha has written a number of books for young readers, including *Failure is Impossible: The History of American Women's Rights*.

In her spare time, Martha sings and plays bass in swing and bluegrass ensembles.

This book is dedicated to my children—Jeff, who is the inspiration for Nick, and Katie, my co-author— Martha E. Kendall

Credits

Author: Martha E. Kendall
Inside Illustrator: Shauna Mooney Kawasaki
Cover Graphics: Peggy Jackson
Project Director/Editor: Mary Rose Hassinger
Editors: Sara Bierling, Kathryn Wheeler
Graphic Layout: Tracy L. Wesorick

McGraw-Hill
Children's Publishing

A Division of The McGraw·Hill Companies

Send all inquiries to:
McGraw-Hill Children's Publishing
3195 Wilson Drive NW
Grand Rapids, Michigan 49544

Printed in the United States of America

Conflict Resolution
ISBN: 0-7424-0180-4

1 2 3 4 5 6 7 8 9 05 04 03 02 01

Table of Contents

Introduction

As children grow and mature, they become more responsible for their lives. As adults make fewer of their decisions, children must begin making choices for themselves. Making these choices is not always an easy process. There are many outside forces that influence the children of today—from parents to peers to television, and more.

Conflict Resolution is a collection of stories in which realistic conflicts are presented and readers are challenged to solve them. In each story, Lisa, a nine-year-old girl, faces a problem typical for a child in elementary school, while her older brother Nick grapples with a more serious version of the same issue. Each story stops before the problems have been fully resolved. The discussion questions provided help readers focus on key elements of the conflicts and prompt students to relate the issues to their own lives. Readers are then encouraged to write and illustrate their own endings.

After the students have created their own conclusions, the provided ending may be read and compared with the students' conclusions. Questions can be presented, such as "What influenced the decisions of the characters? What would influence your decision, in this case? Do facts and/or feelings sway decision-making? Are there right and wrong conclusions? Who sets those standards, if there are any?"

Students will:

* develop critical thinking skills.

* assess the consequences of decisions.

* learn conflict-resolution strategies.

* practice creative writing.

* take control of these stories and their own situations.

* discover that there is more than one right way to finish a story or to solve a problem.

* compare their ideas with those of their classmates and the book.

Using Conflict Resolution

This learner-centered collection of stories may be read in any order and has endless possibilities for presentation and usage. The following are suggested ways of presenting Lisa's and Nick's stories.

✳ Read the beginning of a selected story to the children. You might want to give each child a copy of the story. Or project it as a scanned image or on a transparency for everyone to see. Use the provided discussion questions in small or large groups. Then encourage the students to imagine they are one of the characters.

✳ As part of a conflict resolution curriculum, present stories on a regular basis. After the children gain experience brainstorming and discussing the conflicts involved, have them compose their own endings, identifying situations in their personal lives that remind them of the stories they have finished. If you observe a conflict similar to one dealt with in one of the stories you have already used, ask students how Nick and Lisa would handle it.

✳ When a conflict arises on the playground, at home, or in the classroom, refer to the Topical Index to find a story that deals with the same or a similar issue.

✳ Have students write their own endings to a story. Then, have students read their endings to each other. After they have heard their peers' stories, read the ending provided in the book. Ask students which ending(s) they liked best and why. Discuss the questions listed at the end of the story. To extend the activity, have students write more about one of the discussion topics.

✳ As an alternative, ask for volunteers to write endings in which the characters make bad decisions. Have students determine the consequences of their characters' choices. Then ask the writers to contrast the negative effects of the poor decisions with the positive effects of the good ones noted in the provided ending.

✳ Create or rewrite a story from a new perspective, such as that of Nick and Lisa's parent(s). What problem might they have? What choices are available? Does who we are have an effect on the choices that are available to us? Have students write about it and ask others to suggest good solutions. Children in families that are experiencing difficulties might appreciate this opportunity to consider various ways family members can resolve conflicts together.

✳ Another possibility is to have students write a story about one of Nick and Lisa's friends. For instance, they might write about Jade, who is deaf (in "I Dare You"), Melinda the mean "loser" (in "A Second Chance"), or the "new kid" (in "What Else Is New?").

✳ Have students create their own story endings. Scan the beginnings of these stories and copy them onto your students' computers. Students can then write their endings using their keyboards instead of pencil and paper. Students can also make their own *Conflict Resolution* books. Each child can designate a notebook or journal for this purpose.

✳ For more creative writing practice, invite students to make up their own Nick and Lisa stories, starting not with the ending, but at the beginning. Use a conflict the children are facing to get the plot started. Ask, "What would Lisa do? What similar problem might Nick face, and how would he deal with it? Is it a problem easily solved?"

✳ Instead of focusing on the text of the stories, have students use other media to express their opinions of the decisions made or to show their new stories. The students can paint a beautiful picture of Goldie, draw a portrait of Nick or Lisa, create a cartoon or comic strip using the characters in the Nick and Lisa stories, or create a video skit in which students act out a whole story or scenes from it as well as their new versions and additions. Other options for creative expression would be turning a story into a news article, creating a collage with pictures illustrating the theme or the resolution, or designing a poster stating steps to positive conflict resolution.

✳ You are encouraged to adapt these ideas to suit your students' needs. The most exciting activities relating to these stories, however, may well be those that you and your students create.

The Best

"Lisa, I love your dress!" said her teacher, Ms. Tran. "Is it new?"

"Yes, thank you," said Lisa, smiling.

Lisa turned toward her best friend, Keisha, who sat at the desk next to her. She expected Keisha to give her a compliment, too. But Keisha didn't say anything. She just stared at Lisa's dress. Lisa didn't want to show that her feelings were hurt, so she turned away and began her picture for the art contest. She painted her golden retriever, making careful brush strokes to show the dog's wavy hair. But she doubted her picture could win a prize. Keisha always won.

Just before recess, Lisa asked Keisha, "What did you paint?" Lisa leaned over to look.

"I don't want you to see it," said Keisha, hiding the picture with her hand. She said nothing else. Usually the girls played together at recess, but today Lisa ran to the playground by herself.

That afternoon, when Lisa and her older brother Nick got off the school bus at their stop, Nick said, "Lisa, you look miserable. What's wrong with the Best Dressed Girl in America?"

"Ms. Tran said she loved my new dress, but Keisha just stared at me. I'm so mad I could cry," said Lisa.

Goldie barked, wagged her tail, and trotted over. "Goldie," said Lisa, "I guess you don't care about my new dress one way or the other. How come you're nicer

The Best cont...

than my best friend?"

Nick said, "Goldie wouldn't like it if we got another dog. But she doesn't wish she had a dress like yours."

"That doesn't make any sense," said Lisa. "Just because you're older, you think you can talk in circles."

"No, I don't."

"Yes, you do."

"No, I don't."

"Yes, you do."

Goldie barked, jealous that Lisa and Nick weren't giving her any attention. They laughed and patted her until her body was wiggling as much as her tail was wagging.

The phone rang, and Lisa and Nick raced into the house to answer it. Lisa got there first. She recognized the voice of Nick's best friend.

"It's Kyle," she said, handing the phone to Nick. Then she went into her room to change into jeans and a sweatshirt. Goldie followed along.

"Goldie," Lisa said, "why does Keisha act as if she doesn't like my new dress?" Lisa carefully hung her dress in her closet high enough so that Goldie's tail wouldn't wag against the skirt.

"Actually," said Lisa, "she's acting as if she doesn't even like me!"

Then Nick burst into her room. "Kyle's got a new bike," he said. "I'm going to his house to see it."

Later that night, Nick told Lisa, "I've just got to have a bike like Kyle's. He always gets the best stuff. It's not fair."

"Dream on," said Lisa.

"You got a new dress," said Nick. "I ought to be able to get a new bike."

"My dress was on sale, and bikes are pretty expensive. Besides, Kyle's family is rich," said Lisa.

"I'm so sick of Kyle and his money. Whatever he wants, he gets," said Nick, slamming the door to his room.

The next day at school, Lisa's teacher announced to Keisha that she had won the art contest. "You will be awarded a blue ribbon at the assembly," she explained.

Disappointed that her picture of Goldie had not won a prize, Lisa thought, "Keisha always wins. I wish I could be the best artist at school."

A few minutes later, the teacher held up Keisha's first-place painting so the whole class could see it. Lisa could not believe her eyes! The picture showed Lisa in her new dress.

"The only way I could have a dress as nice as yours," explained Keisha to Lisa, "was if I painted it."

Lisa said, "I have an idea. You like my dress, and I like the way you paint. I'll let you wear my dress at the assembly if you teach me how to paint better."

At recess, the girls talked and giggled about the idea. It felt great to be friends again.

But Nick was not talking to Kyle.

When Lisa and Nick got home from school, Nick grumbled, "I don't even want a bike like Kyle's."

"Yes, you do!" said Lisa.

The Best cont...

"No, I don't," said Nick.

"Yes, you do," said Lisa.

"No, I don't," said Nick.

Goldie barked. "I guess you want some attention, Goldie," said Lisa. Nick tossed a ball for Goldie to fetch. The ball bounced so high it landed on the roof of their mom's car. In a puff of dust, it bounced off the hood.

"That car sure is filthy!" exclaimed Lisa.

"It's been so dry and dusty," Nick said, "everybody's car is gross."

Goldie stood by Nick and Lisa, wagging her tail against the car. Her tail left an arc of bright paint showing where she had wiped off the dirt.

"Goldie," exclaimed Nick, "you've given me an idea!"

Now write an ending. Make it a good one!

Some things to think about while writing:

* What was Nick's idea?

* Does Nick get a new bike? Do he and Kyle become friends again?

* Draw pictures to go with your story.

Here's one good ending to:

The Best

Nick ran into the house and came out with a bucket, a sponge, soap, and a couple of towels.

"I'm starting a car-washing business," he said to Lisa.

He washed their car and put the money his mom gave him in an envelope. Keisha came over and helped Lisa make a beautiful sign, which they set up next to their driveway.

For the next two weeks, Nick washed cars. Lisa and Keisha joined the business, too.

One afternoon, Kyle came by on his new bike. He said, "It's not much fun riding alone, Nick."

Nick said, "Want to join us?"

"Sure," said Kyle. Nick gave Kyle a wet high five, and Kyle squirted Nick with the hose.

"My fingernails have never been so clean before," said Lisa.

"My fingers may never unwrinkle!" Keisha laughed.

"Well, my hands feel great," exclaimed Nick, "because they will soon be on the handlebars of a new bike!"

After several weeks, the car washers took their car wash sign down and went shopping.

Keisha used her money to buy a new dress. Lisa bought art supplies. Nick's mom chipped in so that he could buy a really nice bike.

After the shopping trip Kyle said, "Here's a bike pump and a water bottle for your new bike," and he handed the presents to his best friend.

"Thanks," said Nick.

The girls drew pictures of Kyle and Nick riding their bikes with the best golden retriever in the world running along behind.

Up For Discussion...

Your ending

a. What do you like about your ending to the story?

b. In what ways is it similar to this ending?

c. In what ways is it different from this ending?

This ending

a. If Nick had not earned enough money to buy a really nice bike and his mother could not afford to help pay for it, what other choices might he have had?

b. What do you like about this ending? Is it realistic?

Jealousy

a. What's the difference between liking something that somebody else has, and being jealous?

b. What are some of the negative effects of jealousy? Could there be any good effects of jealousy?

c. Most people feel jealous at one time or another. When was the last time you were jealous? What happened?

d. Do you think any of your friends might feel jealous about something you can do, or about something you own? How could you help them feel better?

The Chase

"Let's chase the girls!" yelled a group of boys. Lisa and her friends screamed, threw their jump ropes down, and darted across the playground. They ran in the direction of some older girls clustered in a circle. The boys gave up their chase when the younger girls joined the bigger group.

Almost out of breath, Lisa tried to peer over the shoulder of one of the older girls. "What are you looking at?" she asked.

"We're not looking at anything," she said. "We're hiding Michelle while she shakes her shirt. She's trying to get a spider off her back. One of the boys shoved it under her collar!"

"Yuck!" exclaimed Lisa. "I hate spiders!"

Michelle finally stood up straight. She had brushed the spider off, but tears still streaked her cheeks.

Just then the school buses pulled up, and everybody ran to board them for the ride home.

Goldie, the family's golden retriever, was waiting at the bus stop for Lisa and her older brother Nick. She jumped up excitedly and gave wet kisses to the children. Nick threw a ball over Goldie's head and yelled, "Chase it!" Goldie wagged her tail and took off after the ball.

"Goldie is smarter than the boys at school!" said Lisa.

"What?" said Nick with a laugh. "You think boys should give drooly kisses and chase tennis balls?" He laughed and tossed the ball for Goldie again.

Lisa rolled her eyes at her brother, and said, "Goldie knows enough to chase balls. Why do the boys always chase us girls?"

"I don't chase girls!" said Nick.

"No, the big boys are even worse! You and your friends put spiders down the girls' backs!" said Lisa.

Now Nick ignored Lisa's comments. Lisa went on, "Just when my friends and I get a good game going on the playground, the boys start chasing us and we have to run!"

"Why?" said Nick. "Does Goldie have to run when I throw the ball?"

"She doesn't have to," said Lisa, "but she likes to."

"Well," said Nick, "if you don't want to run, don't! When the boys say they're going to chase you, don't pay attention." He leaned over and patted Goldie. "You can't chase a ball that's not going anywhere." He tossed the ball, and Goldie leaped after it.

That night Lisa called her friends. "We have to be really brave," she told them. "It's going to be hard not to run when we see the boys coming, but maybe Nick is right. You can't chase something that isn't moving."

The next day when the boys ran toward Lisa and her friends, the girls pretended not to hear them coming.

"Mabel, Mabel, set the table," they chanted as the jump ropes twirled over their heads.

The boys ran closer yelling, "Chase them, chase them."

But the girls paid no attention. The boys yelled again, louder. The girls continued their game.

"This is weird," said one of the boys to his friends. "What should we do?"

"I know," answered another. "Let's go to the soccer field. Kicking the ball around is more fun than running after girls, anyway."

When the boys headed for the field, the girls grinned and changed their jump rope rhyme to, "You can't chase us, we won't run! We like jump rope, we have fun!"

Michelle was so busy watching the younger girls outsmart the boys that she didn't notice Nick's friend Kyle sneak up behind her. But she did notice the slimy feeling of a worm being slipped down her shirt.

When she screamed, Kyle ran to the soccer field. The girls came over to see what had happened. In the restroom, they helped Michelle shake the worm out of her clothes.

Lisa said, "We found a way to make the boys stop chasing us. Now we need to find a way to make the boys stop grossing us out with yucky stuff."

"Why don't we just tell a teacher?" suggested one girl.

"I don't want to be a tattletale," said Michelle. "Anyway, lots of times there isn't a teacher around."

The recess bell rang. Frustrated, the girls came out of the restroom to discover Kyle and Nick carrying a soccer ball back to the PE teacher's office.

Kyle said to Nick, "I hope we have a great team this year."

Michelle heard him and said, "It might be a good team if the players ever practiced with the ball instead of

with bugs and worms!"

The girls nodded in agreement. Kyle said, "Some people just can't take a joke."

At home later that afternoon, Lisa told Nick, "Too bad you're not as good at solving your problems with girls as you are at solving my problems with boys!"

"What do you mean?" he asked

Lisa explained how she and her friends hadn't run away from the boys. "The only bad part was that by the end of recess, we were kind of sick of jumping rope. We're used to being chased by the boys, and we got a little bored without them around."

"Well, I wouldn't miss the girls in my class!" said Nick. "They're always complaining." He phoned Kyle and invited him over to practice soccer.

After a while, they called to Lisa, "We need a third person to practice with us. Want to play?"

For the rest of the afternoon, they dribbled the ball, passed it between themselves, and made goals.

On the bus the next day, everybody was talking about tryouts scheduled that afternoon.

Now write an ending. Make it a good one!

Some things to think about while writing:

* What are the tryouts for?

* Will the boys and girls find an activity they can enjoy together?

* Draw pictures to go with your ending.

Here's one good ending to:

The Chase

Everybody said how much he or she wanted to be chosen for a soccer team. During recess, the boys didn't try to chase the girls. Instead, they practiced passing the ball. Lisa called to her friends, "Let's not jump rope today. Let's play soccer, too."

At first the girls played on one side of the field and the boys on the other. But balls kept crossing the center line and getting mixed up. Finally, Lisa said, "Let's play together."

When the recess bell for the younger grades rang, all the players hated to stop.

When the older kids had their turns playing soccer, Nick and Kyle ran the length of the field, showing off their strong kicks. They paid no attention to Michelle and her friends who talked in a group, watching the boys.

Then Michelle yelled, "Let's go!" The girls stormed the field and kicked the ball away from Kyle and Nick.

"Get it back!" yelled the surprised boys. The girls kept running, dribbling the ball, and passing it between them. Then Michelle kicked the ball through the goal posts.

At the soccer tryouts that afternoon, Nick and Michelle were named co-captains of their team.

"I want Kyle on our team, too," said Nick.

"Only if he promises to play soccer and not to play tricks on the girls," said Michelle.

"It's a deal," promised Kyle later. Lisa and her friends played on Nick and Michelle's team, too. It was named the Retrievers, and Goldie was the chosen mascot. The dog came to every game and watched with envy as the kids chased the ball.

Up For Discussion...

Your ending

a. What do you like about your ending to the story?

b. In what ways is it similar to this ending?

c. In what ways is it different from this ending?

This ending

a. What are some suggestions for how the girls and boys can get along when soccer season ends?

b. What do you like about this ending?

Teasing

a. Why do some people tease others? Is there ever a good reason to tease?

b. Do the boys and girls at your school ever tease each other? Is it fun? If you don't like it, what are some ways you might solve the problem?

Boys and girls

a. Are boys always friends only with other boys, and girls always friends only with other girls? Can boys and girls be friends together, too?

b. What makes a person a good friend?

Compromise

"I don't like that name," said Lisa to the other kids in her group.

"Well, too bad!" said one boy. "I want the name to be the Panthers, and the rest of us do too!"

"I don't," said Lisa's friend Keisha. "I want it to be the Mountain Lions. Don't you, Lisa?"

Lisa knew Keisha wanted her to be on her side, but she didn't like Mountain Lions either. She didn't know what she wanted, except for her group to stop fighting.

Before Lisa could answer Keisha, their teacher, Ms. Tran, walked up to their table and asked, "Have you chosen a name for your booth yet?"

"Yes," said one boy, quickly. "The Panthers."

Two students cheered, but the others yelled, "No!"

Ms. Tran frowned and said, "Every booth at the Autumn Carnival needs a name. Come up with something you all like. You have until tomorrow morning."

The group was still arguing quietly when the bell rang. Ms. Tran said, "Your homework is to think of a compromise. If you can't, then you won't be able to have a booth at the carnival."

After Lisa got home, she told her older brother Nick about her group's problem. She said, "Our

The Compromise cont...

booth is a game. If the player tosses a ball through the hoop, they win an animal toy. But we can't decide what animal to use. This is the hardest homework I've ever had," she said.

Nick said, "It's easy. Call yourselves the Hyenas, and then you can laugh when the people toss and miss!"

"Very funny," said Lisa.

"Or you could be the Vultures and eat everything in sight, which is what I feel like doing right now," said Nick. He followed Lisa into the kitchen.

"I'll make some cookies," she said.

"Great," said Nick. "I'm in the mood for some of those great chocolate cookies."

"But I'm planning to make vanilla cookies with mom's new recipe," said Lisa.

Goldie barked. Lisa turned to her and said, "This is just like talking with my group at school."

Goldie wagged her tail so hard that it knocked against Lisa's cup of flour, spraying a cloud of the white powdery stuff all over Goldie's back.

Nick and Lisa burst out laughing. "Goldie," said Nick, "You're not golden any more. Now you're striped!"

Goldie shook herself off, covering Nick, Lisa, and the kitchen floor with most of the flour that had streaked her back.

"Goldie, you're a genius!" cried Lisa. "Now I know how the kids in my group can compromise."

"Sprinkle each other with flour?" asked Nick with a twinkle in his eye. He reached for the chocolate while Lisa measured more flour.

Lisa explained, "Goldie's stripes are the solution. In my group, some kids want to name the booth the Panthers, which are black, and some want it to be the Mountain

Lions, which are light brown. We can compromise and use an animal that's striped black and brown, like tigers. We could call our game the Tiger Toss!"

Goldie barked, and Nick said, "That's a roar from our own tiger. Goldie wants chocolate cookies just like I do."

Lisa said, "She's roaring at you to compromise. You want chocolate. I want vanilla. Let's make chocolate chip cookies, so we both get what we want."

The next afternoon, Nick grabbed a big handful of cookies as soon as he got home from school.

"You're going to eat all those?" asked Lisa as she took a couple from the jar.

"I need to phone Kyle, and the call may take a long time," said Nick. The nervous smile on Nick's face showed that this was not going to be a regular talk with his best friend.

A long time later, Nick hung up the phone. The cookies were gone, and so was his smile.

Goldie barked and grabbed a ball for Nick to toss.

"I'm not in the mood for games, Goldie," said Nick. "Kyle wants us guys to have a booth at the carnival, but he's being really bossy about it."

"What's the booth?" asked Lisa.

"That's the worst part. He wants it to be the haunted house."

Lisa remembered that two years ago she had been so scared in the haunted house that last year she didn't go near it.

Nick went on, "Kyle's idea is to see who can come up with the best ways to scare the little kids until they cry. I think that's dumb."

"And mean, too," said Lisa, who didn't

want to be considered one of the "little kids" anymore.

"And he says anybody who doesn't like his idea is a sissy," fumed Nick.

"It sounds to me like you need to come up with a compromise, and fast," said Lisa. She hoped they would, because she wanted nothing to do with a haunted house that would make her or her big brother feel like a sissy.

Now write an ending. Make it a good one!

Some things to think about while writing:

* Do Lisa's classmates like her idea of the Tiger Toss compromise?

* Is it possible for Nick and Kyle to work out a compromise?

* If they do, what could it be?

* If Nick and Kyle don't compromise, what might happen at the carnival?

* Will Nick and Kyle get over their argument? How?

* Draw pictures to go with your ending.

Here's one good ending to:

The Compromise

Nick leaned down and patted Goldie's head. "Goldie, yesterday you were a tiger," said Nick. "What can you be today to help me figure out a compromise?"

"If only she could be two things at once," said Lisa.

Nick sighed and rolled the ball across the room. The ball got stuck under a bookcase, so Nick walked around the table and chairs to get it. Then he said, "That's it, Goldie!"

"Goldie chases a ball through the haunted house?" asked Lisa.

Nick paid no attention. He said, "Just like Goldie runs one way and I go another, we can make two different routes through the haunted house. One route for the older students and one for the younger ones," said Nick. "Some stuff could be the same, but we could keep the little kids away from the scariest things."

He ran to the phone to call Kyle.

When the haunted house opened, Lisa stood first in line. Nick and Kyle asked her which side she wanted to try.

Lisa gulped and said, "I want to see the little kids' route first."

Nick opened the door on the left for her. Lisa slowly entered the dark hall. Then she laughed at the smiling skeleton, squeezed the lumpy ghost guts, and giggled at the glowing cats' eyes.

"This is the best haunted house ever!" said one little boy Nick was leading into the door on the left. "Last year I didn't like it, but this year I love it."

Lisa and her friend Keisha got in line together. When they reached the entrance, Lisa said, "We want to try the door on the right."

When Lisa and Keisha exited the haunted house, they were both smiling. They would have gone through again, except it was time for them to take another turn running the Tiger Toss.

Up For Discussion...

Your ending

    a. What do you like about your ending to the story?

    b. In what ways is it similar to this ending?

    c. In what ways is it different from this ending?

This ending

    a. How does it feel to be the youngest?

    b. Have you ever been scared? Talk about it with the group.

    c. Have you ever had a serious difference of opinion with a friend? How did you resolve the issue? Did you both benefit by compromising?

    d. What do you like about this ending?

Compromises

    a. Most families and friends have to work out compromises. Think of a time that you and another person wanted different things. Did you compromise? What was the compromise?

    b. Have you ever watched or read about people who made a compromise? What happened? Describe the steps you took to get to an agreement.

Goodbye

Instead of kicking their feet high in the air, Lisa and her friends sat still on the swings. They did not look happy.

Lisa said, "Maria, you CAN'T move away!" The other girls chimed in, and some of them looked ready to cry.

Maria said, "I don't want to go, but the divorce is final, and we're going to move closer to my grandma."

The bell rang, and the girls headed for their classroom. On their way, Lisa's older brother, Nick, passed them.

He said, "I can't believe you and your friends are all so quiet! Are you trying to win a bet about who can be quietest the longest?"

"Ha ha," said Lisa. "We just found out that Maria is moving away, and we don't want her to go."

"Oh," said Nick. He looked at Maria and said kindly as he hurried to his class, "Bye. I hope you like your new school."

"Your brother is so nice," whispered one of the girls.

"I guess so," said Lisa, "but that doesn't change the fact that Maria is going."

After school, Lisa told Nick, "Thanks for being nice to Maria."

"Well," said Nick playfully, "I was really thinking 'Oh, good, there's one less little friend of yours to bother me,' but it's boring to watch girls cry, so I didn't say it." Then he laughed, jumped out of her reach, and ran out the door.

Goodbye cont...

"You're AWFUL!" Lisa yelled as she leaped after him, laughing in spite of herself.

The phone rang all afternoon. Lisa's friends were trying to decide what to do about Maria's moving. As Lisa talked, she sipped a big mug of hot chocolate. She thought to herself, "I feel bad, but this sure tastes good."

"I've got an idea," she said to one of her friends. "Maybe we can make something good happen because of this. Let's ask Ms. Tran if our class can have a party for Maria, and we'll all tell about our favorite times with her."

The next day, Lisa discussed her idea with Ms. Tran, who liked it very much. She said, "Many of you have been classmates with Maria ever since preschool. I'm sure you have lots of memories to share."

When Nick saw Lisa and her friends on the playground that day, they were talking excitedly about the party. "Now you sound back to normal," he said.

"Well, it won't be normal without Maria in our class, but at least we'll have fun saying goodbye to her."

"We're not going to have fun saying goodbye in our class," said Nick.

"Who are you saying goodbye to?" asked Lisa.

"We just found out that Ms. Anderson has cancer. Next Friday will be her last day as our teacher's aide. She has to start her treatment." He hesitated a moment and then added, "Maybe she'll never come back."

"Oh, Nick, that would be terrible. Everybody loves Ms.

Anderson! I've been looking forward to working with her, too."

"If it weren't for her, I think I'd be failing math," said Nick. "If I make a mistake, she turns the problem into a game. When I finally understand how to do it, she tosses me her eraser so I can fix my answer. I have a collection of her erasers."

"What are you going to do when she leaves?" Lisa asked.

For once Nick had nothing to say. In fact, Lisa thought he might actually cry.

Now write an ending. Make it a good one!

Some things to think about while writing:

* What might Maria's party be like? Will children be both happy and sad?

* Is there anything Nick and his class can do for Ms. Anderson?

* Draw pictures to go with your ending.

Here's one good ending to:

Goodbye

After Maria's party, Lisa talked about the fun everyone had.

Then Lisa added, "Maybe your class can have a party for Ms. Anderson."

"I don't think we have much to celebrate," said Nick. Then he turned to Goldie, "Let's go outside," he said. "I'll toss the ball for you."

In the back yard, Goldie leaped in the air even before Nick released the ball from his hand. Nick laughed and said, "Goldie, it's almost like you and this ball are connected."

Goldie ran after the ball and brought it back to Nick again and again. "Oh gross," he said, "Your slobber is covering this thing!"

When Nick and Goldie went back inside, Lisa said, "When you left, you looked miserable. What are you smiling about now?"

"Goldie's drool-covered ball gave me an idea for Ms. Anderson. I'm going to suggest that everyone in the class gives something to Ms. Anderson that is related to our class."

"What has that got to do with Goldie's ball?" asked Lisa.

"When I look at that ball, I think of Goldie," Nick said. "When Ms. Anderson looks at our stuff, it will help her think of us."

Nick told Ms. Santos his idea. She liked it.

The class made Ms. Anderson a book to go with the gifts they chose for her. After reading it, she said, "I'll read these stories often. They'll make me feel like you are all with me." She paused and then she added, "I want to feel like I'm with you, too. I will keep the book, but I would like each of you to save the gifts. They'll help you to remember me."

After school Lisa asked Nick, "What did you bring?"

"I showed an old eraser and told about how Ms. Anderson helped me turn wrong answers into right ones. Then she gave me something." Nick held up a new eraser and smiled. "She said to make this last until she comes back. You can bet I'll try!"

Up For Discussion...

Your ending

    a. What do you like about your ending to the story?

    b. In what ways is it similar to this ending?

    c. In what ways is it different from this ending?

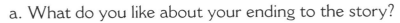

This ending

    a. Do you think Maria liked her party? Why?

    b. Can writing letters help maintain friendships?

    c. Do you think Ms. Anderson appreciated her book and gifts?

    d. What other objects and stories do you think the students had for Ms. Anderson?

    e. What do you like about this ending?

Connections between people and objects

    a. Do you think an object can remind you of a person? Give an example of how.

    b. Describe an object you have that reminds you of a special person.

Saying goodbye to friends

    a. Has a friend of yours ever moved away? How did you feel?

    b. Have you moved from one school to another? What part of the experience was hard for you? Were there any good parts? What made the change easier?

    c. Do you write letters to anyone?

Death

    a. Have you known someone who died? Did you have a chance to say goodbye?

    b. Are there memories you have about that person that make you feel good when you think about him or her? How will you remember him or her?

Crying

    a. Have you ever been embarrassed about crying? Tell about that time.

    b. Do you think Nick should feel embarrassed for feeling so badly about Ms. Anderson and her illness and leaving the class? Why or why not?

    c. How should you react when you see someone crying?

"I Dare You"

"I didn't want to do it!" said Lisa, almost in tears. "But everybody was yelling at me and laughing. I had to!"

"What did you do?" asked her brother Nick.

"I stood behind Jade, the deaf girl, and said every bad word I know. The other kids called me a goody-goody because I wouldn't do it at first."

"Since Jade is deaf, she doesn't even know what you said, Lisa," said Nick.

"Jade's interpreter wasn't around, so you're right; Jade doesn't know what I said. But my teacher, Ms. Tran, heard me," said Lisa. "She told me she was disappointed in me."

"Don't worry," said Nick. "Remember that saying 'sticks and stones will break my bones, but words will never hurt me'? Did Ms. Tran give you a detention or anything?"

"No," said Lisa.

"Then there's no problem," said Nick.

"That's what you think," answered Lisa. "I feel terrible." She went to call her friend Keisha.

Nick heard Lisa ask Keisha, "Why did you and everybody else want me to be so mean to Jade?"

When she got off the phone, Nick asked her, "What did Keisha say?"

"She said everybody teased her to do the same thing, too."

"Who is 'everybody'?" asked Nick.

"Everybody but us!" said Lisa. "And they're supposedly our friends!"

"Some friends," said Nick.

Lisa ran to her room, and Goldie followed along.

"At least you don't make me do things I don't want to do," said Lisa, "except when you want me to let you out and I'm feeling too lazy." Goldie wagged her tail. "That's okay, Goldie," said Lisa. "You're only a dog."

The next day, Lisa and Keisha stayed away from their other friends. They sat with Jade at lunch, and Jade's interpreter helped them communicate with her.

"Are there bad words in sign language?" Lisa asked Jade.

"You bet," Jade said through her interpreter.

Ms. Tran saw Jade, Lisa, and Keisha laughing together when they came to class. She winked and smiled at Lisa.

But Nick wasn't smiling later that afternoon.

"Why are you so happy?" he growled at Lisa.

"I don't feel guilty anymore about Jade," she said. "Why are you so unhappy?"

"I think I may have some big trouble," Nick said.

"Uh-oh," said Lisa. "What did you do?"

"The other guys and I were hanging out by the Snack Shack," he said, "and somebody said, 'I dare you to grab some candy.'"

"What happened?" asked Lisa.

"Everybody started taking stuff. I felt weird about it, so I backed off. A guy who's kind of a bully grabbed a huge handful of candy. Then he said, 'I dare you to take something.' The other guys laughed, and I didn't know what to do. I thought about running away, but all my buddies were there. So, I quick grabbed a candy bar. Then I heard a grownup's voice say, 'Nick, what are you doing?' The other guys took off, but my feet wouldn't move."

"Who caught you?" Lisa asked.

"It was one of the mothers who supervises the Snack Shack. I said I really wanted to buy the candy bar. She said it looked like I was going to steal the candy."

"What did she do?" asked Lisa.

"She told me she's responsible for the Snack Shack this week, and there will be a big problem if candy and money are missing," said Nick.

"What's going to happen to you?"

"She said she doesn't want us to get into trouble, but she'll have to tell on us if we don't pay. But she doesn't know the names of the other guys. She only caught ME."

"What are you going to do?" asked Lisa.

"I'm going to find a way to get all the guys to bring the candy back or pay for it. That way maybe nobody will get into trouble," said Nick.

"How are you going to manage that?" asked Lisa.

"I don't know," said Nick, "but I better figure something out soon."

Now write an ending. Make it a good one!

Some things to think about while writing:

* Will Nick get the other boys to bring the stolen candy back to the Snack Shack? What might happen to them if they do go back?

* What might happen if Nick can't get them to go back?

* Draw pictures to go with your ending.

Here's one good ending to:

"I Dare You"

At school the next morning, Nick saw the boys who had taken the candy. He said, "You guys all took off from the Snack Shack yesterday, but the supervisor saw you. You have to bring the candy back."

"I can't," each one said. "I already ate it."

"Come talk to the supervisor with me," said Nick. "I think she'll help us find a way to stay out of trouble."

By the end of the day, all the boys agreed to Nick's idea, except for the bully, who refused to come.

"Then you have a major problem," Nick told him.

"Oh yeah? What?" the bully said.

"The supervisor knows a lot of guys took stuff. If all the missing candy isn't paid for, I think she'll make us tell her everything that happened and exactly who was there," said Nick.

"You wouldn't dare!" the bully snapped.

"You want to bet?" said Nick, trying to sound more confident than he felt. "If we don't, we'll be blamed for what you took."

The bully scowled, but he trailed along behind the other guys. When the boys reached the Snack Shack, the supervisor asked, "Do you have the missing candy?"

"We ate it," they confessed.

"What do you think is the fairest way to handle this?" she asked.

"Well, we probably should pay for it," said Nick's best

friend Kyle.

"Definitely," said the supervisor. Then she added, "It's not okay to take something, but I understand that everyone makes mistakes. Stealing is a crime, though, and I think to make up for it you need to do more than just pay for the candy."

"Maybe we could work a shift at the Snack Shack, too," suggested Nick.

"That's a good idea," said the supervisor.

The boys agreed to the plan. They paid what they owed, and they each took a turn in the Snack Shack that week, too. Even the bully did his share.

One guy joked when Nick came in to help, "I dare you not to take anything."

"No problem," said Nick.

At the end of the shift, he took nothing with him but a smile and a sigh of relief.

Up For Discussion...

Your ending

a. What do you like about your ending to the story?

b. In what ways is it similar to this ending?

c. In what ways is it different from this ending?

This ending

a. Did Lisa do the right thing when she talked to Jade at lunch?

b. How do you think Jade felt about their conversation?

c. Do you think the boys' punishment was fair?

d. What do you like about this ending?

Using inappropriate language

a. Are there certain words that you are not supposed to say?

b. Why are some words not appropriate at any time?

c. How do you feel when you hear friends use inappropriate words?

Taking a dare

a. Why do some people dare others to do things?

b. Has anyone ever dared you to do something? Did you do it? Why or why not?

c. Can other people MAKE you do something you do not want to do?

d. Can peer pressure ever be a good thing?

Bullies

a. Do you know any bullies?

b. What happens to people who stand up to bullies?

Stealing

a. Do you know anyone who has stolen something? Was that person punished?

b. Have you ever been caught taking something that wasn't yours? What was the punishment, and do you think the punishment was fair?

c. Was something of yours ever stolen? How did you feel? Did you get the stolen item back?

Left Out

After the final bell rang, Lisa and her friends crowded around the school bulletin board. Girls shrieked with delight: "I've got the lead!" "I'm in the chorus!" "I'm a dancer!"

"Lisa, what are you going to be?" asked her friend Keisha. Lisa studied the list of students selected for the play, but her name wasn't there.

"Nothing," said Lisa. "I didn't get chosen."

"Oh, no," said Keisha, "that's terrible." The other girls chattered with Keisha about the first rehearsal, and they all scurried away to find the director of the show.

Lisa walked to the school bus by herself.

Her older brother, Nick, sat down in the seat in front of her. "What's up?" he asked.

"Nothing," said Lisa. "Well, I didn't get picked for the play, and everybody else did."

"Who wants to be in some dumb show, anyway?" he said. "All those rehearsals would be boring."

Nick's friend Kyle sat down next to him and they started talking about baseball. Lisa stared out the window for the whole ride home.

Goldie barked to welcome Nick and Lisa as they got off the bus. But she ran along with Nick and his friends when they rode their bikes to the field to play baseball. "Now I don't even have my dog to talk to," moped Lisa.

That evening, and every night that week, Lisa's

Left Out cont...

phone hardly rang. Lisa's friends called the other girls in the play to talk about play rehearsal.

"Have a peanut butter cookie," Lisa said to Nick one afternoon when he got back from playing ball.

"Thanks," he said, taking three of them. "These are great. You should make some more."

"I might as well. There's nothing else to do while all my friends are in the play," she said. "But I'd rather be with them than trying cookie recipes."

"Well then, why don't you?" asked Nick.

"Why don't I what?" asked Lisa.

"I don't know," said Nick with a wink, "but I bet you can figure it out." He dropped a handful of cookies into a bag and called to Goldie, "Let's go back outside!"

"Big help you are!" mumbled Lisa as she watched Nick and Goldie join some of Nick's friends in the yard. Nick offered cookies to his buddies, and they gobbled them up.

"A cookie break! Perfect!" exclaimed Lisa to herself.

The next afternoon, Lisa got her mother's permission to ride her bike back to school. She carried a big bag of freshly baked sugar cookies. During rehearsal breaks, Lisa talked with her friends and offered them cookies.

"These are great! Thanks!" the kids exclaimed. "Come to all the rehearsals," Keisha said. Then she told Lisa about the play and the funny mistakes they made during rehearsals.

"It's not all fun, though," one girl said. "It gets boring when we have to wait for our turn on stage. But now we can look forward to your coming."

Left Out cont...

When Lisa got home, Nick ate the last cookie and asked, "Do you have any more?"

Lisa smiled and said, "I gave them to the kids in the play. I'm going to make more cookies for next week."

"Great," said Nick. "Bring some to the baseball team, too. Tryouts are on Monday, and then the team will practice every day."

"Okay," said Lisa. She pulled out the cookbook and searched for more recipes.

But Monday afternoon, after Lisa returned from the play rehearsal, Nick came home looking miserable. He did not want a cookie. "I blew the tryouts," he said. "I didn't make the team."

He hurried to his room and closed the door. Goldie whimpered in the hallway, and Lisa said, "I know how Nick feels. But I don't think baking cookies will help him feel any better."

Now write an ending. Make it a good one!

Some things to think about while writing:

* What might Nick do to feel better about not making the team?

* Is there anything Lisa can do to help her brother?

* Draw pictures to go with your ending.

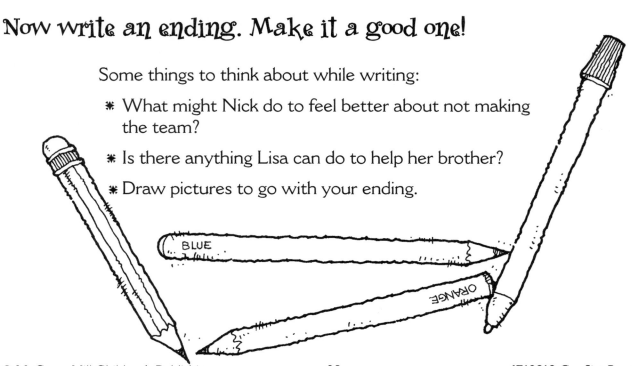

Left Out

The phone rang, and Lisa recognized the voice. It was Nick's best friend Kyle.

Before she called Nick to the phone, Lisa asked Kyle, "Did you make the team?"

"Yes," Kyle answered. "Nick is the only good player who didn't make it."

Lisa handed the phone to Nick. During his conversation, she heard him say, "I know" a dozen times, and then he hung up.

"What were you telling Kyle that you know?" asked Lisa.

"I know the team needs me!" he said. "I think I can play as well or better than most of the guys who were picked, but I definitely know I understand the whole game more, how to practice, and how to organize the gear. The team will be a mess without me to keep everything straight!"

"Tell that to the coach," said Lisa.

"He'll just think I'm a bad loser," said Nick.

"Let's go to practice together tomorrow," said Lisa, "after the play rehearsal. We can bring cookies to the guys. I know they'll like the oatmeal ones I just learned to make."

"What have your cookies got to do with me helping the team?" asked Nick.

"I don't know," said Lisa with a wink, "but I bet you can figure it out."

"Big help you are!" mumbled Nick as he started his homework. Lisa just smiled and put a bookmark in the cookbook.

The next afternoon, she baked an extra batch of oatmeal cookies. Then she and Nick rode their bikes to school.

Lisa gave cookies to the kids in the play. Keisha smiled and showed her the program for the opening performance. There was Lisa's name as Cookie Break Coordinator!

Nick watched the baseball practice. Then Lisa took the remaining cookies over to the ball field. As soon as she arrived, the players begged the coach to let them have a short cookie break. While the team sampled the treats, Nick talked to the coach.

"I know I didn't make the team this year as a player," he said, "but I think I can help in other ways. I'm good at organizing the gear, and I'm friends with everybody on the team. I can remind them about stuff to bring, times to be at warm-up sessions, and help in any other ways you want."

The coach said, "Nick, I really wanted you to be part of the team, but you just didn't play very well at the tryouts. Next year you'll probably make it. As far as this season goes, I like your suggestions. Why don't you be our team manager?"

"You bet," said Nick.

Nick ran over to the guys and told them the news. "I'm the manager," he said, "and my first direction to you is to have another cookie!"

Everybody laughed, and Lisa distributed all the cookies she had brought.

As she and Nick rode their bikes home, Lisa thought about new recipes, and Nick thought about ways he could help the team prepare for their first game.

Nick and Lisa both felt like winners, and that's just what they were.

Up For Discussion...

Your ending

a. What do you like about your ending to the story?

b. In what ways is it similar to this ending?

c. In what ways is it different from this ending?

This ending

a. Do you think Nick will make a good manager?

b. What are the differences between being a player and being a manager who helps the players perform at their best?

c. Have you ever acted in a play or worked backstage on a show? Which role would you prefer? Why?

d. What do you like about this ending?

Failure

a. Have you ever tried out for something but not been accepted? What did you learn from the experience?

b. Is it possible to always get what you want?

c. Have you ever tried for something even though you doubted you would get it? Why did you take that chance?

d. What can you do to feel better when you do not get what you want?

Being alone

a. Have you ever felt bored and lonely by yourself? What are some things you can do to feel better?

b. What makes people feel like outsiders? What can you do to help them feel that they belong? What can they do to help themselves?

Not a Thief

Mr. Jacobs, a new substitute teacher in Lisa's class, passed out a math quiz. He said, "I'm going to give each of you a calculator to use. When you hand in your quiz, you must return the calculator. Anyone who does not return their calculator will receive a detention."

"I don't like him," Lisa whispered to her friend Keisha.

"No talking during the quiz!" boomed Mr. Jacobs.

Lisa squirmed. Every time Mr. Jacobs looked at her, she got more nervous. She couldn't concentrate on her quiz.

The lunch bell rang, and the other students ran outside. Lisa still had two problems to finish.

"I hope he doesn't yell at me again," she thought.

Another teacher came to the room to see Mr. Jacobs, and while they talked, Lisa finished the problems. Then, as fast as she could, she darted from the room.

At lunch, her friend Keisha asked her, "What's that in your pocket?"

"Oh, no!" said Lisa. "It's Mr. Jacobs' calculator!"

"Wow," said Keisha. "He's going to think you stole it!"

"I'm not a thief!" Lisa answered.

"What's that I just heard?" asked Lisa's older brother Nick. He and some friends were walking toward the sports field. Nick carried the school's bag of baseball equipment.

Not a Thief cont...

"Somebody thinks you're a thief?" he asked.

"I didn't mean to take it!" said Lisa, almost in tears.

Nick groaned and rolled his eyes at Lisa.

"It's simple," he said. "Whatever you took, just give it back." One of his buddies added, "Or if it's something good, give it to one of us!"

Lisa mumbled to herself, "It's not so simple, Mr. Know-It-All."

At the end of the day, she still had the calculator in her pocket.

When Nick and Lisa got off the bus they were surprised that Goldie wasn't there to meet them.

"Maybe she's chasing some poor, helpless kitten," joked Nick.

"Maybe she did something wrong and she's hiding," said Lisa.

When Nick and Lisa got to their home, Goldie greeted them with her friendly bark. Mom had forgotten to let Goldie out, so she was stuck inside the house at the time she usually met the kids at the bus stop.

"Well, I guess you're not guilty of anything!" said Nick as Goldie jumped around, wagging her tail excitedly. He grabbed playfully at her flopping ears.

Lisa walked to her room and set the calculator on her desk.

"I wish I'd never seen this calculator," she thought to herself. "I wish I'd never seen Mr. Jacobs, either."

Goldie trotted down to Lisa's room. "Goldie, I'm glad you're not in trouble," said Lisa. "One of us is enough."

Nick called from the kitchen, "Goldie, let's play ball."

"No," said Lisa. "She's keeping me company right now."

"Why are you hiding in your room? You must have done something really bad."

"Why does everybody always make me out to be guilty of things?" said Lisa.

"I was just kidding," said Nick. "When you act like you're guilty, people are going to think you're guilty. Did you tell your teacher about the calculator?"

"No."

"Look," said Nick. "I'm going to take a bike ride to school and throw the ball around for Goldie. You can come too, and give the calculator back to Mr. Jacobs. The longer you wait, the more he's going to think you just wanted to keep it."

"What if he yells at me? What if he says I'm a thief and I get kicked out of school?"

"If you don't return the calculator, then you WILL be a thief," said Nick.

Nick and Lisa got their mother's permission to ride their bikes to school, and Goldie ran along with them.

"Oh, no," said Lisa when they got there. "Mr. Jacobs is talking to the principal, and she doesn't look happy. I hope Mr. Jacobs isn't reporting me!"

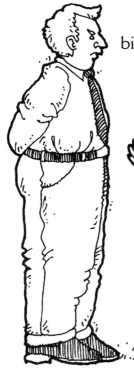

The principal and Mr. Jacobs stopped talking when Nick and Lisa rode up. Lisa's heart was pounding so hard she could barely take the calculator out of her pocket.

"Mr. Jacobs," Lisa said, "I'm really sorry. I was so worried about finishing the quiz after the bell rang that I just forgot to turn in this calculator. It's been in my pocket all afternoon."

"So you're the one who didn't return the calculator," said Mr. Jacobs.

"I didn't want anybody to think I stole it, so I came back to school to give it to you," Lisa said.

The principal smiled at Lisa and said, "I sometimes lose track of things, too. I'm glad you brought the calculator back, Lisa. I'm sure Mr. Jacobs feels the same way."

"Definitely," he said.

Just as Lisa breathed a sigh of relief, the principal looked at Nick and said, "You are the one who has some explaining to do."

"What do you mean?" asked Nick.

"Didn't you have the baseball equipment out today?"

"Yes."

"Well, it's gone. You were the last person to sign it out, and it has not been checked back in. Those balls, bats, and gloves are worth a lot of money," she said. "Nick, did you bring them back?"

Flustered, Nick mumbled, "I don't know, I'm not sure."

"Well, I hope you can remember, and soon," said the principal.

Now write an ending. Make it a good one!

Some things to think about while writing:

* Do you think Nick actually stole the equipment? What might he have done with it?

* If he doesn't have it, how might he find it?

* Draw pictures to go with your ending.

Here's one good ending to:

Not a Thief

Lisa and Nick rode off on their bikes.

"Where is the bag, Nick?" Lisa asked.

"I don't know!" said Nick.

"Did you put it away after lunch recess?" asked Lisa.

Nick paused. "When the bell rang, I think I forgot about the bag. I just ran to my class. I guess I might have left it in the field."

"Then it should still be there, right?"

Nick and Lisa hurried to the field, with Goldie following closely alongside them. The bag was nowhere in sight.

"I HAVE to find it," said Nick.

Goldie barked. "Sorry, girl," said Nick. "No playing ball with you now."

Nick walked around the edges of the field.

"The bag's not here," he told Lisa. "I'll check the gear closet in the gym. Will you see if anybody turned it in at the lost and found?"

They met back at the field ten minutes later. "No luck," they both said.

It was starting to get dark, so they rode their bikes home. On the way, Nick said, "Maybe one of the guys picked it up."

That night Nick called every boy that had played baseball that day. The ones who answered the phone said they didn't know anything about the missing bag. He left messages for the guys who didn't answer. Nick's mom suggested that he and Lisa make signs to put up around the school. Each sign said: "Lost—bag containing school baseball equipment. Please return to the principal."

Just before lunch recess started the next day, the principal called Nick to her office.

"Have you found the baseball equipment?" she asked.

"I think I left it in the field," said Nick. "I just forgot to put it away. I didn't steal it!"

"How can I help you find it?" she asked him.

"I don't know," said Nick. "Can I make an announcement over the school PA system to see if anybody knows where it is?" asked Nick.

"Sure," she said. "That's a good idea."

Nick said to everyone at the school, "The school's baseball equipment has been lost. We believe it was left on the west ball field. If anybody has any information about it, please report it to the office as soon as possible."

As soon as the bus dropped Nick off at home, he got his mother's permission to ride his bike back to the school to look for the gear bag once more.

Nick searched the field again, looking in the trees surrounding the field this time. At the base of one pine tree, sat the equipment bag! All of the equipment was still inside it.

Nick grinned from ear to ear. He carried the bag to the principal's office.

"Good for you, Nick," she said. "You made a mistake when you forgot to return the bag right away. But you worked hard to find it, and I'm proud of you."

When Nick got home, he threw a ball for Goldie to retrieve.

"It's taking you FOREVER to get that ball!" he called to her as she searched the hedges where the ball landed.

Finally she carried it to him. "Good job, Goldie," said Nick. "Like me, you manage to bring things back."

Up For Discussion...

Your ending

a. What do you like about your ending to the story?

b. In what ways is it similar to this ending?

c. In what ways is it different from this ending?

This ending

a. Do you think the principal really thought Nick had stolen the gear?

b. Do you think Nick learned a lesson? What was it?

c. Should he be punished for forgetting to put the gear away?

d. How do you think the gear bag ended up by a tree near the field?

e. What do you like about this ending?

Losing things

a. Have you ever lost something important? Did you find it, or did someone else find it?

b. Did anybody ever think you purposely did something wrong, when it was really just an accident? How did that feel?

c. If you lose something, what are some ways you can try to find it?

d. Have you ever found something valuable that was not yours? What happened?

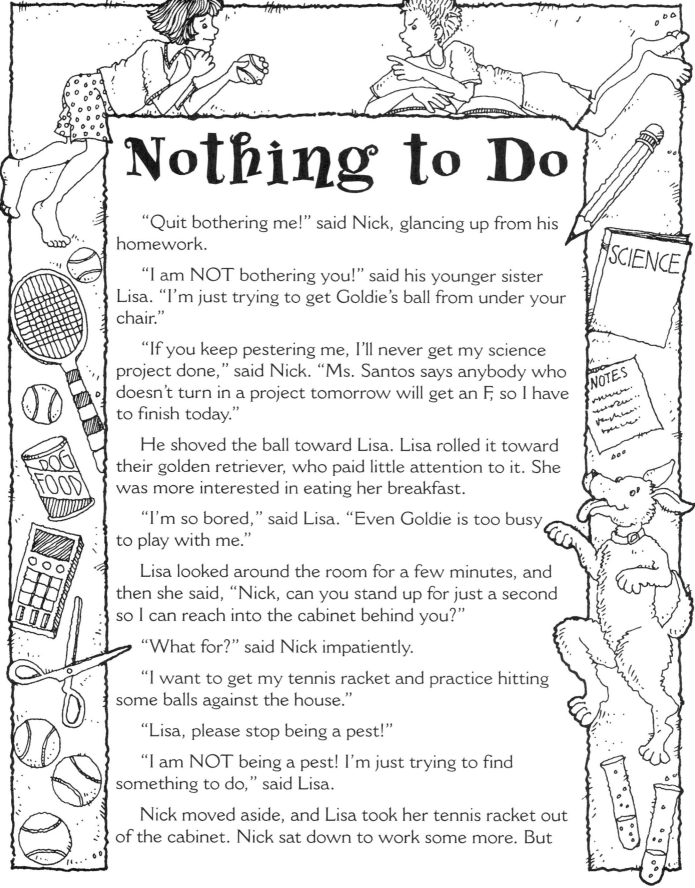

Nothing to Do

"Quit bothering me!" said Nick, glancing up from his homework.

"I am NOT bothering you!" said his younger sister Lisa. "I'm just trying to get Goldie's ball from under your chair."

"If you keep pestering me, I'll never get my science project done," said Nick. "Ms. Santos says anybody who doesn't turn in a project tomorrow will get an F, so I have to finish today."

He shoved the ball toward Lisa. Lisa rolled it toward their golden retriever, who paid little attention to it. She was more interested in eating her breakfast.

"I'm so bored," said Lisa. "Even Goldie is too busy to play with me."

Lisa looked around the room for a few minutes, and then she said, "Nick, can you stand up for just a second so I can reach into the cabinet behind you?"

"What for?" said Nick impatiently.

"I want to get my tennis racket and practice hitting some balls against the house."

"Lisa, please stop being a pest!"

"I am NOT being a pest! I'm just trying to find something to do," said Lisa.

Nick moved aside, and Lisa took her tennis racket out of the cabinet. Nick sat down to work some more. But

Nothing to Do cont...

soon he heard a thud, thud, thud.

"Lisa," he yelled out the window. "I can't concentrate on my project when all I can hear is that ball hitting the house! Instead of bothering me, find something else to do, will you?!"

Lisa sighed and called Goldie to her. "Well girl, can you help me find something to do?"

Goldie looked up at Lisa. "Ugh," Lisa exclaimed. "You have dog food breath! You're useless!"

Goldie gave a soft bark. Lisa giggled. "I'm sorry, Goldie. You're not useless. That's the first time I've laughed all day. I guess you are useful." Keeping her nose away from Goldie's mouth, Lisa gave her dog a hug, and Goldie wagged her tail. "Maybe I can stop being bored if I find a way to be useful, too," said Lisa.

Lisa went inside and asked Nick, "Could you use my help on any part of your science project?"

Nick thought a moment. "Sure," he finally said. "I added up all the numbers on the report really late last night, and I might have made some mistakes. Can you check them with your calculator?"

Lisa ran to her room to get her calculator, and Goldie bounded along behind her, sliding right past the doorway on the slippery floor. Lisa laughed again and raced Goldie back to the family room where Nick was working.

Lisa found mistakes, and Nick corrected each one.

"I'm glad we fixed those," said Nick. "But Ms. Santos will probably fail me anyway. She's been acting pretty mean lately."

"Of course, I know you are absolutely perfect," said Lisa with a twinkle in her eye. "Why is Ms. Santos mad at you?"

"She says my friends and I are always hanging around outside her classroom making noise after school. About every five minutes she yells out the window for us to be quieter."

"Why do you stay there, then?" asked Lisa.

"Her room is next to the bike racks. You know the principal's rule. Nobody is allowed to ride bikes around school until after 3:00, so all we can do is sit around and talk. What's wrong with talking to each other while we wait?"

"What's wrong is that Ms. Santos is mad at you," said Lisa. "Good luck getting an A when you turn your paper in tomorrow."

The next afternoon, Nick was late getting home.

"Where's Nick?" Lisa asked her mother.

"Ms. Santos called to say Nick would be staying later than usual after school today," she answered.

"Uh-oh," thought Lisa. "He must really be in trouble."

Now write an ending. Make it a good one!

Some things to think about while writing:

* Why do you think Ms. Santos asked Nick to stay after school?

* Does Ms. Santos have the right to be annoyed with Nick and his friends for hanging around and making noise outside of her classroom?

* Should Nick try to do something to please Ms. Santos? If so, what?

* Draw pictures to go with your ending.

Here's one good ending to:

Nothing to Do

Nick got home from school just before dinner. Goldie was so happy to see him that she leaped up to greet him.

"Lisa," Nick laughed, "did you just feed Goldie?"

"If you can laugh about Goldie's dog food breath, something good must have happened to you today," said Lisa.

"After school, Ms. Santos yelled at us again. She said she was trying to grade our reports, but couldn't concentrate because of us. She was holding my report in her hand, and she looked mad. I told her I was sorry, and I asked her if I could help with anything.

"Ms. Santos actually smiled! She asked me if I would check off the names of the people who had turned in their reports. While I did that, I heard Kyle and the guys fooling around. So I asked Ms. Santos if there was anything all of us could do to help her.

"She said our next science unit was on transportation, and she had storage boxes filled with supplies in the closets behind the cafeteria. She asked us to carry the boxes to the display cases in the hall. All the guys helped. Then Ms. Santos asked us to unpack the boxes and arrange the things for display. There was a lot of neat stuff, like old-fashioned wheels, model rockets, and a remote control steamboat. Then Ms. Santos told us we can earn extra credit if we make a bulletin board display showing how bikes work. It's going to be fun!"

"Time for dinner," called Mom.

As Nick and Lisa walked toward the dining room, Nick said, "After dinner I'll start cutting pictures of bikes out of magazines."

"My homework's all done. Could you use some help?"

"You bet," said Nick.

Up For Discussion...

Your ending

a. What do you like about your ending to the story?

b. In what ways is it similar to this ending?

c. In what ways is it different from this ending?

This ending

a. Why did Ms. Santos finally smile at Nick?

b. Do you think the boys enjoyed carrying the supplies and arranging them in the display cases?

c. Is it fair that they will get extra credit for making a bulletin board display the next day?

d. What do you like about this ending?

Having nothing to do (boredom)

a. Have you ever been so bored you could not think of anything to do? Can you think of some specific times that has happened to you?

b. When you are bored, what are some things you can do?

c. Can you give examples of times you have enjoyed helping other people?

d. Has anybody ever made you feel unwanted or that you were bothering them? What did you do?

e. Has somebody ever pestered you?

f. What's the best way for you to tell someone to leave you alone?

A Second Chance

When Nick got on the school bus for the ride home, he didn't say hello to his younger sister Lisa. Instead, he and his friends talked about their new PE teacher.

"Mr. Johnson is completely unfair," complained Nick.

"I think he's a total jerk!" said Nick's friend Kyle.

"Let's tell the principal how bad he is," said another boy.

After Nick and Lisa got home Lisa said, "What's so bad about Mr. Johnson?"

Nick said, "He thinks he's a hot shot. He shows off. He did twenty-five push-ups, and when we tried, he just laughed at us."

"Are you really going to tell the principal?" asked Lisa.

"We should," said Nick. "I don't like him at all."

"Why don't you beat him at push-ups?" asked Lisa.

"Oh, sure," said Nick, rolling his eyes.

"I bet I can do twenty-five!" said Lisa. She hopped down onto the floor and began. Goldie trotted over and started licking Lisa's face. Lisa burst out laughing.

"I wish Goldie could come to our PE class," said Nick.

The next morning, Nick and his friends talked to the principal about Mr. Johnson.

She said, "He's a brand new teacher here. Tell him when you think he's not being fair. Give him a chance."

During PE class that day, Mr. Johnson told the students

to run one mile. He said anybody that didn't finish would have to stay after school.

"I don't think that's fair," said Nick. "If we try our hardest, that should be good enough."

"Let's see you try then," said Mr. Johnson. He laughed and called out, "I'll race you!"

He took off running and Nick and the other students followed. Mr. Johnson crossed the finish line well ahead of everyone else. When the warning bell rang Nick, Kyle, and only a few others had also crossed it.

Mr. Johnson jogged back onto the track to join the slower students for their last lap.

One of boys said to Nick, "Trip the teacher!"

"Yeah, do it!" said Kyle.

"Trip him, trip him," chanted the others.

Nick stuck his foot out but he pulled it back at the last second. Mr. Johnson saw him.

"Nick, you stay after school!" Mr. Johnson yelled. The final bell rang and Mr. Johnson said, "Everybody else is excused. See you tomorrow."

"Good luck, Nick," said Kyle as he ran to catch the bus.

"Nick, why did you nearly trip me?" demanded Mr. Johnson.

"Because the guys told me to," said Nick.

"Why did you change your mind?" asked Mr. Johnson.

"Because I didn't want to get in trouble," said Nick.

"Well, you are in trouble," said the teacher.

Nick blurted, "You're the one who should be in trouble!"

"What do you mean?" said Mr. Johnson.

"Why do you always laugh at us?" Nick asked. "PE isn't fun anymore!"

Mr. Johnson looked surprised. "Why?"

"It's fun to be able to do things, but you make us feel stupid and uncoordinated," said Nick.

Mr. Johnson thought a moment. "Maybe I have been too hard on you all."

Then he turned to Nick and said, "I appreciate your telling me how you feel." He shook Nick's hand.

"Thanks, Mr. Johnson," said Nick.

When Nick got on the late bus to ride home, he was surprised to see Lisa and a group of her friends on it, too.

"Why did you stay after school?" he asked them.

"Because of Melinda, the Loser!" they said. "She is really mean. She walks around telling everybody they're ugly, or stupid. So today when she got on a swing we circled her and called her a loser."

"What's that got to do with your staying after school?" asked Nick.

"Ms. Tran gave us all detention," said Lisa.

"What happened to Melinda?" asked Nick.

"She walked past us while we were stuck in detention. She made a face at us and laughed," said Lisa.

"What are you going to do about it?" asked Nick.

"I don't know yet," said Lisa, "but we'll figure something out."

Now write an ending. Make it a good one!

Some things to think about while writing:

* Why might Melinda be so mean?

* Can the girls do anything to make Melinda stop?

* Draw pictures to go with your ending.

Here's one good ending to:

A Second Chance

At lunch the next day, Lisa said to her friends, "Let's do a disappearing act. Whenever Melinda comes near us, we'll take off. Then she can't be mean to us, because we won't be there!"

Melinda ate lunch by herself. When she passed by the girls' table on her way to throw her trash out, the group of girls stood up and headed in the other direction. They didn't even look at her.

A few minutes later, when Melinda walked toward the swings, Lisa's group turned around and ran to the monkey bars.

Just before the bell rang, Lisa and the other girls stopped at the restroom. They were surprised to find Melinda there. She wasn't being mean or calling people names. She was crying.

"What's wrong with you?" Keisha asked, still angry about yesterday's fight.

"I hate you!" shouted Melinda.

"Why are you so mean to us?" snapped Lisa.

"Because you're always mean to me!" said Melinda. "You are always together, talking and laughing. I'm always by myself. That makes me feel bad."

"You make us feel bad when you say mean things!" said Lisa.

"I don't want to be called a loser. I want to have some friends," said Melinda.

Lisa and her friends didn't say anything.

"I'm sorry I said mean things to you. Please give me a chance," said Melinda.

The bell rang, and the girls filed out of the restroom.

Melinda was holding the door for them. Just as Lisa was about to pass through, she stopped and held the door for Melinda. As Melinda passed through the door Lisa said, "We'll try if you do, Melinda. I think we can all be friends as long as we work on it together. You go ahead."

"Thanks," said Melinda with a smile.

The principal was standing in the hall by the restroom.

"My goodness, it must have been crowded in there!" she exclaimed as she watched the girls come out.

"We're a growing group," said Lisa.

The girls all giggled, including Melinda.

Up For Discussion...

Your ending

a. What do you like about your ending to the story?

b. In what ways is it similar to this ending?

c. In what ways is it different from this ending?

This ending

a. Did Lisa and her friends do the right thing when they avoided Melinda?

b. Do you think Lisa and her friends will accept Melinda into their group?

c. What do you like about this ending?

Being mean

a. Has anyone ever been mean to you?

b. Why did that person act that way?

c. How did you treat that person in return?

d. Has anyone ever called you mean? Why?

e. Have you ever been mean to someone on purpose?

Groups or cliques

a. Do some students always play with the same group of friends?

b. Are outsiders welcome to join the group?

c. Have your friends ever urged you to do something that might get you into trouble? Did you do it? What happened? If you didn't do it, why didn't you?

Forgiveness

a. Everybody makes mistakes. How did Mr. Johnson discover he had made a mistake? Do you think he will change? Will Nick and his friends give him a chance?

b. Have you ever given a second chance to a teacher, friend, or family member who made a mistake?

c. Have you ever been given a second chance?

Secrets to Tell

"I want blueberry. What flavor do you want?" asked Lisa. She and her friend Keisha stood next to each other in the line for ice cream cones.

"I want vanilla," Keisha said. Then she asked, "Can you keep a secret?"

"Sure," said Lisa.

Keisha whispered, "Here's the secret. Megan said something mean to me, so I took her new blue pencil box. You know, the one with the flower designs on it? Don't tell her."

Lisa felt her stomach go flip-flop. Then she said, "I don't think I want any ice cream after all." She headed for the playground.

Most days, Lisa ran to the swings. She and Keisha liked to swing next to each other, pumping their legs at the same time so that they could go back and forth together. Today Lisa dragged her heels as she crossed the blacktop. She thought to herself, "Keisha and Megan are both my friends. I wish I had never heard that secret."

The first person Lisa saw on the playground was her older brother Nick. Without using her friends' names, she told him what had happened.

"I think you should tell the one who stole the pencil box to give it to me!" Nick said. He laughed and joined a game of catch that had just started.

"Big help he is!" thought Lisa.

During afternoon recess, Lisa kept away from both

Keisha and Megan. She didn't know what to say to either of them.

When Lisa got home, Goldie barked and greeted her with a wet kiss. "Want to go for a walk?" asked Lisa. Goldie answered by jumping up and wagging her tail so fast that it nearly whipped everything off the coffee table.

"Goldie," said Lisa as they walked along, "I don't know what to do. I promised Keisha I would keep her secret. I can't go back on my word. But she stole Megan's favorite pencil box. Megan is my friend, too. I feel like I should help get her pencil box back."

Goldie cocked an ear. Then she turned around and barked. Nick was coming.

"Oh, great," thought Lisa. "Nick will be even less help than Goldie."

"Hi, Lisa," said Nick. "Guess what?"

With a twinkle in her eye Lisa teased, "You got the prize for being the world's worst brother?"

"Very funny," said Nick. "Your problem about the stolen pencil box is nothing compared to my problem."

"Oh, yeah?" she said. But Nick looked worried. Lisa asked, "Do you need some help from the world's greatest sister?"

Nick began his story. "Kyle was throwing a baseball around, practicing his pitch," he said.

"What's so special about that?" said Lisa.

"His grip slipped, and the ball hit the plant by our classroom door. The pot broke. It was the fancy one Ms. Santos brought back from her trip to Japan. I was the only one on the playground to see it happen, and Kyle

Secrets to Tell cont...

begged me not to tell anybody. But what do I say tomorrow if Ms. Santos asks the class if anyone knows how her pot was broken?"

Goldie started barking, and Nick smiled. He ruffled the back of Goldie's head and teased, "Goldie, if you know what I should do, quit barking and tell me!"

"That's it!" said Lisa. "Goldie's just given us the answer. Maybe she can't talk, but we can. I'll talk to Keisha about the pencil box. It's not fair for her to ask me to keep a secret that she stole something from another friend of ours." Lisa looked at Nick. "Maybe you should talk to Kyle too," she said.

"I don't know," said Nick, shaking his head. "Kyle is my best friend. I don't want him to think that I'm not on his side."

"But do you really want to lie if Ms. Santos asks about what happened?" asked Lisa.

"No," said Nick with a sigh. Slowly he added, "I guess I'll call Kyle. No matter what he says, I can't feel worse than I do now."

"I'll race you home!" yelled Lisa. They ran as fast as they could, but Goldie easily beat them. By the time Lisa and Nick reached the back steps, Goldie had taken a huge drink of water, most of which she slobbered all over the children in excited kisses.

"Yuck," said Lisa. "Telling Keisha how I feel is not going to be easy, but it will be better than getting drowned in dog drool."

Lisa called Keisha. Then Nick called Kyle.

"Well?" they asked each other.

Lisa began. "Keisha couldn't even remember what supposedly mean thing Megan had said to her. She promised to go to school early and put the pencil box back in Megan's desk," said Lisa. With a smile, she added, "She asked me to play on the swings with her tomorrow." Then she paused and asked, "What did Kyle say?"

"Kyle said he would call Ms. Santos. But he didn't sound like he wanted to. I don't blame him."

Nick still looked worried. He grabbed his baseball and bat. Goldie jumped up and followed him outside. Nick tossed the ball in the air, swung his bat, and hit the ball across the yard.

"Goldie, go get it!" Nick yelled. Goldie ran almost as fast as the ball she was chasing. Time after time, she brought it back to him.

"Nick, phone call for you!" called Lisa from the house. She recognized Kyle's voice. "I hope he's not mad at Nick," she thought as she handed him the phone.

Now write an ending. Make it a good one!

Some things to think about while writing:

* Do you think Kyle will call Ms. Santos? What might he tell her, and what might she say?

* If he does not call her, what will he tell Nick? What might he do instead?

* Draw pictures to go with your ending.

Secrets to Tell

After Nick hung up, he looked as happy as if he had just hit a home run. He said to Lisa, "You'll never believe this! Ms. Santos saw the whole thing from the classroom window. She knew Kyle had broken the pot, and she was waiting for him to admit it. If he hadn't told her the truth, Ms. Santos was going to report him to the principal. And then he might not have been allowed to play on the baseball team this year."

"What about the broken pot?" asked Lisa.

"I don't know. I didn't ask him that. But Kyle invited me over this Saturday. We'll practice pitching and batting for the first game of the season."

That night at dinner, their mom asked, "What did you learn at school today?"

"Not much at school, mom," said Lisa. "But after school, Goldie taught us something."

"What do you mean?" she asked.

Nick said, "Dogs can bark, but people can talk."

Mom gave them a funny look. Lisa and Nick smiled, and Goldie's tail pounded the floor.

Up For Discussion...

Your ending

a. What do you like about your ending to the story?

b. In what ways is it similar to this ending?

c. In what ways is it different from this ending?

This ending

a. What do you think Kyle expected Ms. Santos to say?

b. Do you think he did the smart thing by calling her? Why?

c. Kyle broke Ms. Santos's pot. What do you think he should have to do to make up for it?

d. What do you like about this ending?

Secrets

a. Have you ever been asked to keep a secret?

b. If somebody asks you to keep a secret that makes you feel uncomfortable, what can you do about it?

What Else Is New?

When Lisa got off the school bus, she told her older brother Nick, "I have a problem."

"So what else is new?" he said. They walked to their house, with their golden retriever trotting along next to them.

"This is a new problem," she said.

"You want to get something new and Mom says no?" asked Nick.

"Very funny," said Lisa. "Everybody is supposed to tell a true story to the class. Everyone thinks it will be fun, but I don't want to do it."

"It will be easy," said Nick with a smile. "Tell them about the time you gave Goldie a haircut and she looked like a mutant poodle."

Lisa rolled her eyes and said, "Choosing a story is not the problem. I don't want to have to stand in front of the class by myself. It makes my stomach go flip-flop just thinking about it."

"Tell the class about the time you threw up after riding on the roller coaster. Then if you feel sick, you can do a demonstration," said Nick.

Lisa ignored her brother's comment. She tossed a ball for Goldie, who leaped into the air and caught it in her mouth after one bounce.

"Goldie," said Lisa, "I remember when you were a puppy and you tripped all over yourself when you tried to fetch a ball. I feel like I'll trip just walking to the front of the class before I even start my speech."

Nick threw a stick in the air. "Let's see if Goldie can fetch a stick as well as she catches the ball," he said.

His first toss landed in the oak tree, but he found another stick and tried again. He threw it high in the air, and Goldie let out a yelp of surprise when the stick landed on her back.

"I think you could both use some practice," said Lisa, laughing. Then her expression changed to worry. What if her classmates laughed at her when she told her story?

Goldie barked. Then Lisa said, "That's it!"

"You're going to bark instead of talk when you tell your story?" said Nick.

Lisa said, "Just like you and Goldie have to practice throwing and catching the stick, I will practice giving my talk."

Nick said, "I bet Goldie would love to listen," and he headed inside to answer the phone.

Lisa said, "Goldie, you don't look much like my friends in class, but here goes." She got so involved telling Goldie a story that she hardly noticed when Nick returned.

He said, "That was the new kid in my class. He invited me over on Saturday afternoon."

"Are you going?" asked Lisa.

"Yes," said Nick. "I'm not sure I want to, but I couldn't think of an excuse, so I said I would."

"Why don't you want to?" asked Lisa.

"He seems kind of different,"

 IF19212 *Conflict Resolution*

said Nick, "and the other guys won't hang out with him. But his desk is next to mine, so I have to be nice to him."

"I hope the class is nice to me when I give my speech tomorrow," said Lisa. "I'll die if they make fun of me."

All evening she told her story to Goldie. Just before she went to bed, Lisa said, "Goldie, I'm still nervous about tomorrow, but I think I'm as ready as I'll ever be." Goldie wagged her tail, and Lisa fell asleep.

The next afternoon on the school bus, Lisa's friend Keisha said, "I loved your story today, especially the way you told about teaching Goldie to fetch."

"I had fun telling it," said Lisa, thrilled that her practice paid off so well. "I thought I could never stand up in front of the whole class but I pretended I was talking to a room full of Goldies!"

The real Goldie greeted Nick and Lisa at their bus stop. Lisa said, "Goldie, let's practice some more with the stick."

While she and Goldie played, Nick checked the mail. He pulled out an envelope addressed to him. "It's an invitation to Kyle's birthday party," he said, frowning.

"You don't look very happy about it," said Lisa.

"It's on Saturday afternoon at the same time I said I'd go over to the new kid's. Now I'm going to have to miss my best friend's birthday party just because I made the mistake of being nice to the new kid!"

"Maybe Kyle invited him, too," said Lisa.

"No way," said Nick.

"Why don't you call Kyle and ask him to invite the new kid?" said Lisa.

"I don't know how much I like him. I'm not going to ask Kyle to invite him because I say so, and then have him turn out to be weird!"

Frustrated, he threw a ball high into the air. It landed in the top of the oak tree.

"What are you going to do?" asked Lisa.

"I don't know what I'm going to do about the new kid," said Nick. "But as for that ball, I'm going to try to knock it loose."

He threw a big stick into the tree, but it landed nowhere near the ball. Lisa threw another stick into the tree, but hers missed the ball, too. Then someone rode up on a bike.

Nick whispered to Lisa, "It's the new kid."

Now write an ending. Make it a good one.

Some things to think about while writing:

* What might the new kid say and do?

* Should Nick still go to the new kid's house on Saturday?

* Should Nick make up an excuse and go to the birthday party instead?

* Should Nick ask Kyle to invite the new kid to the party?

* Make pictures to go with your ending.

Here's one good ending to:

What Else Is New?

"Hi," said Lisa. "Do you have a name besides 'the new kid'?"

"Sure," he said. "I'm the world's greatest retriever."

Goldie barked, and the boy said, "I'll get that ball down."

He threw a stick up and hit the ball, knocking it to the ground. Then he tossed the ball between his legs to Goldie, who leaped up and caught it.

He smiled and asked, "Do you have any more balls?"

Lisa handed him two more. The new kid started juggling. He bent over and tossed them through his legs, behind his back, high, and low. Goldie jumped excitedly as she watched the balls fly through the air.

"That's fantastic," said Nick.

"Thanks," said the new kid. "Well, I'll see you tomorrow at school." He rode off on his bike.

At school the next day, Nick told Kyle about the new kid's juggling. Kyle said, "I'll invite him to the party and ask him to show us his tricks!"

On Saturday afternoon, Nick and the new kid rode their bikes to the party together. Soon, everybody wanted to learn how to juggle.

Kyle said, "Nick, thanks for telling me about the juggler."

Riding their bikes home later, Nick asked his new friend Peter, "How did you get so good?"

"Practice," he answered.

When they pulled into Nick's driveway, Peter, the world's greatest juggler, tossed a stick for Goldie. She missed it the first time. He threw it again, and she caught it perfectly.

Up For Discussion...

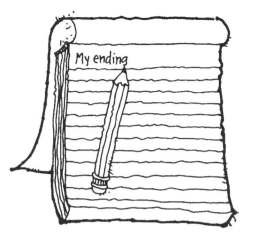

Your ending

a. What do you like about your ending to the story?

b. In what ways is it similar to this ending?

c. In what ways is it different from this ending?

This ending

a. In some ways, the new kid seemed different from Nick's other friends. It turns out that one of his differences, his ability to juggle, made him popular. Choose someone you are getting to know. What makes that person different from your other friends?

b. What makes you special?

c. Peter says he became a good juggler because he practiced. Tell about a time when practice made a difference in your life.

d. Why do you think Nick's friends avoided the new kid? Do you think it's natural to feel suspicious of new people or things? Why or why not?

Trying new things

a. Have you ever been the new kid at school, at camp, or in your neighborhood? What did it feel like?

b. Can you think of a time you were nervous about trying something new like diving into a swimming pool or eating an unusual food?

c. How can you help yourself feel better about trying new things?

d. Is it always good to try new things?

e. Can you remember trying an activity for the first time and thinking it was really hard, but then practicing it until it became easy for you? Give as many examples as you can.

Who Did It?

"Have you finished your story yet, Keisha?" asked Lisa. The two girls sat next to each other on the school bus.

"Yes, but it's not very good," said Keisha.

"Oh, I'm sure it is," said Lisa. "You're a great writer."

"Not as good as you," said Keisha.

"You're much better," said Lisa, trying to make her friend feel good.

"Well, then," Keisha said slowly, "let's trade stories. If mine really is as good as yours, it won't make a difference."

Lisa gulped, unable to think of anything to say. She exchanged stories with Keisha.

That day in class, Ms. Tran asked the students to read their stories aloud. When Keisha read the story Lisa had given her, everyone laughed and clapped.

When Lisa's turn came, the class was looking forward to a good story, for hers were always the best. But when Lisa finished, nobody said anything. The story had been boring.

Keisha and Lisa did not sit with each other on the school bus that afternoon. Keisha turned away when Lisa and her older brother Nick got off at their stop.

"What's wrong with the World's Two Best Friends?" asked Nick.

"I tried to make Keisha feel good," said Lisa, "but now I feel bad."

Goldie barked, and Nick said to their golden retriever, "Maybe you can understand her. I sure can't."

Lisa explained to Nick what had happened.

"What does Keisha say about it?" he asked.

"I don't know," said Lisa. "She hasn't talked to me since we read the stories."

"Well, I may need a good story for tomorrow," said Nick, "but not one that's written down."

"What do you mean?" asked Lisa.

"I did something right, but I'm the loser," he said.

Now Lisa said to Goldie, "Maybe you can understand him. I sure can't."

Nick explained. "Groups in my class are supposed to make a model of a volcano. The group that makes the best one gets to have ice cream during last recess. My group's was the best until another group brought their project in today."

"Why was that one better?" asked Lisa.

"One of the girls in that group said that her father could make a better model than the group could. Her father made one, and the group turned it in like they had done it. It's much better than my group's," said Nick.

"That's not fair! Tell the teacher!" said Lisa.

"How?" said Nick. "Ms. Santos gave us a big speech about being good losers. If anybody says that group didn't do their own model, they'll say we're bad losers. We lose no matter what," said Nick, slamming the door to his room.

Lisa went outside to play fetch with Goldie. She tossed

the ball, but it landed in the gutter on the garage roof.

"Oops!" cried Lisa. She called to Nick, "I need your help! Will you get the ball?"

Nick came out and stretched to reach into the gutter of the garage roof. Lisa exclaimed, "That's it! Now I know what to do about my problem with Keisha."

"You're going to throw your next story onto the roof?" asked Nick.

"Very funny," said Lisa. "Just like I needed your help to get the ball, Keisha could use my help writing a story. I'll ask my teacher if Keisha and I can work together on the next one."

The phone rang and Nick answered it. "I don't recognize the voice," he said, "It's a grownup."

After the call, Lisa said to Nick, "That was Ms. Tran!"

"What did you say?" asked Nick.

Lisa's voice shook a little when she said, "I told her I wanted to help Keisha, and I knew I didn't do it the right way. She said she understood, but that she couldn't give Keisha or me credit for the stories. She liked my idea of us working together on the next story. She said she'd give us a grade on that one. She's calling Keisha now."

Nick said, "You're lucky. I wish my teacher would figure out which group didn't make their own model."

Now write an ending. Make it a good one!

Something to think about while writing:

* Is there some way Nick can show that the other group didn't do their own project and not seem like a bad loser?

* Draw pictures to go with your ending.

Here's one good ending to:

Who Did It?

Nick put Goldie's dinner in her bowl, but Goldie didn't run to gobble her food as she usually did. Instead, she slowly walked up with her tail between her legs. Smeared on her face were the leftovers from Nick's lunch bag, which she had just eaten.

"Guilty!" said Nick. "But thanks, Goldie. You've given me an idea."

"You're going to eat Goldie's dinner?" asked Lisa.

Nick paid no attention to his sister's comment. "Goldie's face showed what she did. Maybe that group at school will somehow show what they did, too."

The next day in class, Nick raised his hand and said, "I think each group should explain how they made their volcano. Our group will start." Each person in his group described what part he or she had done to complete the project.

When it was time for the group that had not made their own to come forward, none of the students could think of anything to say. They had no idea how the student's father had made it.

Then Ms. Santos said, "The group that couldn't explain how they made their model must do another one after school. And the prize for the best volcano goes to Nick's group. Enjoy your ice cream."

When Nick and Lisa got off the school bus, Goldie was waiting for them. Nick opened his lunch bag and said, "Goldie, I saved this extra cup of ice cream for you." Within moments, Goldie had a vanilla mustache and a tail that wouldn't stop wagging.

Up For Discussion...

Your ending

a. What do you like about your ending to the story?

b. In what ways is it similar to this ending?

c. In what ways is it different from this ending?

This ending

a. The group that cheated was given a chance to make its own volcano. Do you think the students should have been punished?

b. Do you think Nick's idea was a good one? Can you think of another way his problem could have been resolved?

Cheating

a. Do you know of any times when students have turned in or copied somebody else's work instead of doing their own? What happened?

b. What should you do if you see someone cheating?

c. Cheating is against school rules and the law. Why do you think it is considered such a bad thing?

d. What should you do if you don't think your own work is good enough?

e. Is cheating at a sport or a game different from cheating on schoolwork?

f. Do you think that people who are guilty always look guilty? Why or why not?

Topical Index

For more information on Conflict Resolution:

Community Boards
1540 Market Street, Suite 490
San Francisco, CA 94102
phone (415) 552-1250
fax (415) 626-0595
e-mail cmbrds@conflictnet.org
www.communityboards.org

* Neighborhood-based conflict resolution program that trains members of the community in effective communication, mediation, problem-solving, and other related skills.

Creative Response to Conflict, Inc.
Box 271
521 North Broadway
Nyack, NY 10960
phone (914) 353-1796
fax (914) 358-4924
e-mail CCRCNYACK@aol.com
www.planet-rockland.org/conflict/

* Program providing school and community-based workshops in which activities help children experience new ways to examine conflicts and develop solutions.

Educators for Social Responsibility
23 Garden Street
Cambridge, MA 02138
phone (800) 370-2515
fax (617) 864-5165
e-mail educators@esrnational.org
www.esrnational.org

* Provider of educational resources and professional development for educators, parents, administrators and community members who seek to create caring and cooperative learning environments

ETR Associates
PO Box 1830
Santa Cruz, CA 95061-1830
phone (831) 438–4060
www.etr.org

* Publisher of books and pamphlets about nonviolent conflict resolution and good health practices for teens and pre-teens.

Office of Juvenile Justice and Delinquency Prevention (OJJDP) of the Department
of Justice
810 Seventh Street NW
Washington, D.C. 20531
1–202–307–5911
fax 1–202–307–2093
e-mail askjj@ojp.usdoj.gov

OJJDP's Juvenile Justice Clearinghouse
P.O. Box 6000
Rockville, MD 20849-6000
1–800–638–8736
fax 1–301–519–5212
e-mail askncjrs@ncjrs.org

* published guide to be used as a tool for strategic planning and implementation of a
   conflict resolution program

* includes reading and resource lists

* videos also available

National Association for Community Mediation
1726 M. Street NW
Suite 500
Washington, D.C. 20036
1–202–467–4769
fax 1–202–466–4769

* listings of community mediation centers

Safe and Drug-Free Schools Program
US Department of Education
Washington, D.C. 20202
1–202–260–3954
e-mail safeschl@ed.gov

* information on establishing conflict resolution programs

Children's Literature Bibliography

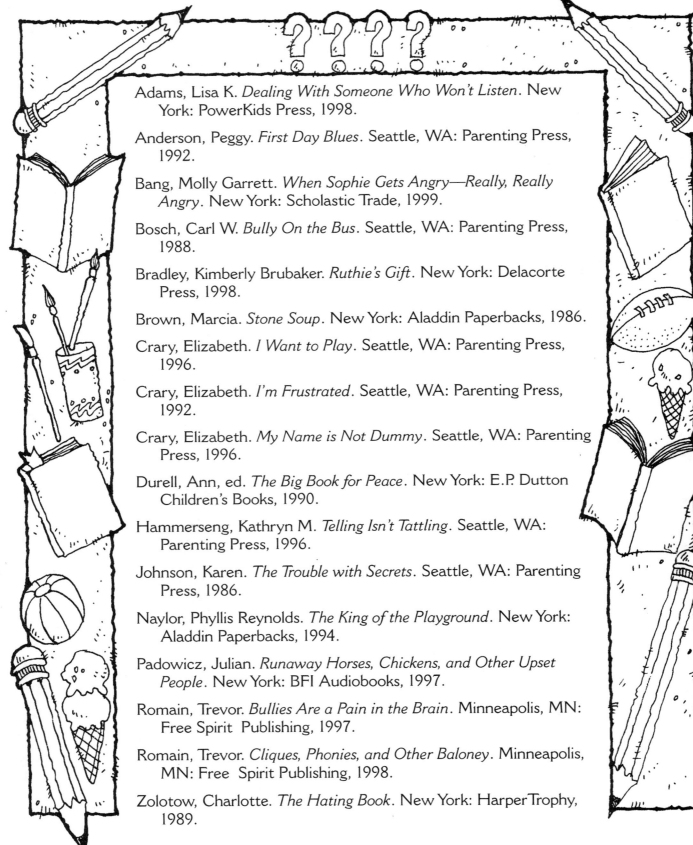

Adams, Lisa K. *Dealing With Someone Who Won't Listen*. New York: PowerKids Press, 1998.

Anderson, Peggy. *First Day Blues*. Seattle, WA: Parenting Press, 1992.

Bang, Molly Garrett. *When Sophie Gets Angry—Really, Really Angry*. New York: Scholastic Trade, 1999.

Bosch, Carl W. *Bully On the Bus*. Seattle, WA: Parenting Press, 1988.

Bradley, Kimberly Brubaker. *Ruthie's Gift*. New York: Delacorte Press, 1998.

Brown, Marcia. *Stone Soup*. New York: Aladdin Paperbacks, 1986.

Crary, Elizabeth. *I Want to Play*. Seattle, WA: Parenting Press, 1996.

Crary, Elizabeth. *I'm Frustrated*. Seattle, WA: Parenting Press, 1992.

Crary, Elizabeth. *My Name is Not Dummy*. Seattle, WA: Parenting Press, 1996.

Durell, Ann, ed. *The Big Book for Peace*. New York: E.P. Dutton Children's Books, 1990.

Hammerseng, Kathryn M. *Telling Isn't Tattling*. Seattle, WA: Parenting Press, 1996.

Johnson, Karen. *The Trouble with Secrets*. Seattle, WA: Parenting Press, 1986.

Naylor, Phyllis Reynolds. *The King of the Playground*. New York: Aladdin Paperbacks, 1994.

Padowicz, Julian. *Runaway Horses, Chickens, and Other Upset People*. New York: BFI Audiobooks, 1997.

Romain, Trevor. *Bullies Are a Pain in the Brain*. Minneapolis, MN: Free Spirit Publishing, 1997.

Romain, Trevor. *Cliques, Phonies, and Other Baloney*. Minneapolis, MN: Free Spirit Publishing, 1998.

Zolotow, Charlotte. *The Hating Book*. New York: HarperTrophy, 1989.